Christian Motorcyc

By John Pickering

The author aged two, with his brother David, on their dad's
BSA 1000cc side-valve

First published in Great Britain in 2024 by John Pickering

ISBN: 9781445774992

Copyright Year: 2024

Copyright Notice: John Pickering. All rights reserved.

The above information forms this copyright notice:

© 2024 by John Pickering. All rights reserved.

Photographs used in this publication have, except where indicated, been taken by the author.

Cover image designed by Mark Hamilton © 2024

Christian Motorcycle Maintenance

Introduction

This book is short and simple. It's based on a diary I kept at the time. After unearthing this old, battered document I found that it contained the basic foundations of a book. I had to rely on my memory to construct the rest of the story.

You may not agree with the Christian content but the ideas and philosophy in the text are easily understood. This book is not intellectually challenging or highbrow. It is a true story of two close friends on a short motorcycle road trip around Scotland in the early seventies. One of the friends, that's me, begins to see the spiritual aspect of the journey, whereas the other friend, that's Mick, is not affected in this way.

If you are particularly anti-Christian, you could skip the religious bits and just read about our journey. However, I don't recommend this method. Please read it as a whole, and I hope my reflections will help you in your personal journey through life. One of Mick's famous quotes was "All my life I have striven for the goal of mediocrity. I hope, with God's help, to one day achieve it."

Mick's self-deprecating humour may amuse us, but nevertheless the truth is that most of us only attain mediocrity as far as this world's system goes. I truly believe that God wants our lives to be much more than mediocre. He wants us to have lives that are meaningful and of a higher quality than that which the shallow modern media and advertisement world portray.

Jesus said, "I have come that they may have life, and have it to the full". (John 10:10)

To use the motorcycle analogy, you have two cylinders in life. One is physical and one is spiritual. To have a full life you need to be running on both cylinders.

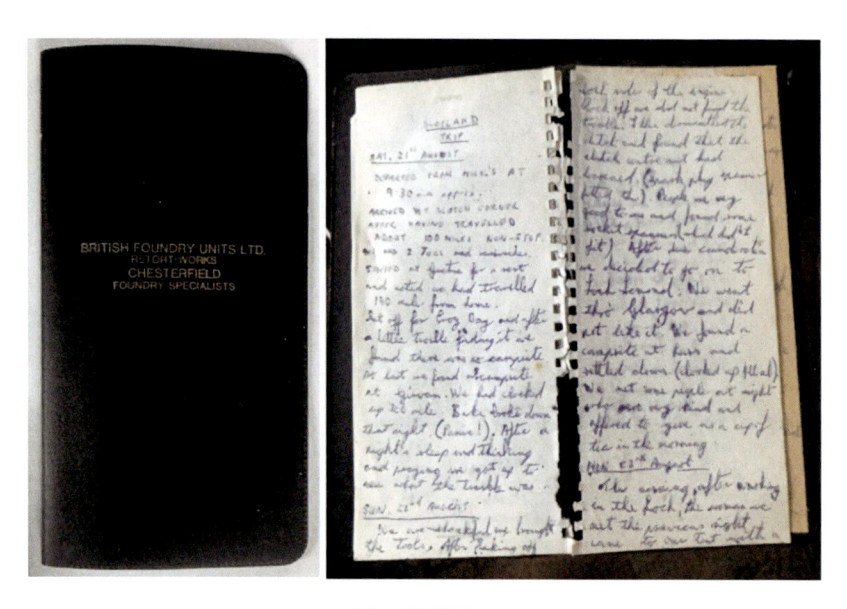

The Old Diary

Chapter One

I woke up that morning and felt very excited. Going outside I took a good look at the bike. I'd packed my stuff on the rear rack the previous night and had checked the oil level, tyre pressure etc. She was looking good. Her chrome gleaming in the morning sunshine. Her red and black paint cleaned and polished.

My Trusty Steed – Royal Enfield Crusader Sports

After breakfast I put on my riding gear. Levi jeans, Levi shirt and my treasured Lewis Leather biker jacket. The outfit was completed with sturdy boots, open face helmet, goggles, and leather gloves.

I said goodbye to my mother and told her I would be away for a few days and not to worry. The look on her face told me she was worried already. Like countless mothers throughout the world, she was always worried when her boy was out on the bike.

Stepping outside I turned on the petrol tap and tickled the carb. She started second kick, as always, and the sound of the single cylinder 250cc engine heralded the start of an adventure. Sitting astride the machine, this collection of metal, rubber and plastic felt alive. I was John Wayne, and this was my faithful steed. I was Steve McQueen, and this was my Great Escape.

I let her warm up for a few minutes and then turned off the choke. Everything sounded good so I engaged first gear and set off towards Mick's house. Mick Collins was one of my closest friends and he had been given the privilege of riding pillion on this road trip. Mick quickly stowed his stuff on the back of the bike and then with difficulty slid himself between me and the tower of luggage. We both shuffled around to get comfortable and realised it was a tight squeeze. Fortunately, we were both skinny eighteen year olds, but nevertheless we were concerned at the prospect of travelling hundreds of miles so tightly packed together. It was a good job that we were close friends.

As soon as we set off up the road, we realised there was a serious problem. At slow speed the front wheel was wobbling like crazy, and I had to wrestle with the handlebars to get any control. As we increased our speed the wobbling stopped, and we were running smooth. As we slowed down the wobbling started again.

We pulled to a stop to investigate the problem. My first thought was that the front wheel was loose, but I soon found that the wheel nuts were tight and there was no movement in the bearings. Mick and I had both been on the bike the day before without any problems. So, what was different today? It was obvious; the pile of luggage on the back was levering the front end up and causing a wobble at low speeds.

So, what could we do about it? We had only taken the bare minimum of stuff. One tent, two sleeping bags, one change of clothes each, soap and small towel and a few tools. We both decided that each item was essential. We had tried sleeping rough before without a tent and it never worked well. There was only one thing we could do. We couldn't jettison any of the stuff and we couldn't rearrange it, so I would have to learn the new skill of riding a wobbly machine at slow speeds and hope most of the journey I could open up the throttle and break through the "Wobble barrier".

I realise this sounds dangerous (and it was) but we were young and just wanted to get on with the adventure. As teenagers, health and safety were not our priorities. So, for hundreds of miles, I wrestled with the handlebars every time we slowed down. That trip really toned up my arm muscles.

We had a general idea that we were heading up to Scotland. Neither of us had been north of the border before and we were looking forward to visiting some of the famous places. However, the fact is we weren't really bothered about specific destinations. We just wanted to keep riding and experience the joy of the open road on two wheels.

I was grateful that most of the first day was spent on the A1. Mostly it was a straight dual carriageway where we could maintain speeds of 50 to 60mph. Our first stop was at Scotch Corner. We had travelled 100 miles without a break and our backsides were killing us. My bike was not made for comfort and the constant vibrations and bumps had taken their toll. After dismounting we both stretched our legs and massaged our bum muscles. We then had mugs of tea and sandwiches in the café. After discussing the journey so far, Mick and I made a rule that from now on we would stop every 50 miles or so and give our buttocks a break. This turned out to be a good decision; the short breaks freshened us up and our rear ends never suffered agony for the rest of the trip.

As we emerged from the cafe, we noticed one old man standing next to the bike. He told us that he was an ex-biker and how much he envied us.

"Make the most of being young lads. It doesn't last forever. Soon you'll be an old codger like me who can't even get on a bike."

We both laughed. We could never imagine being old like him. However, we both decided to take his advice and make the most of being young. One day as old men we would still be talking about this trip. Re-living those glory days and still laughing about all the crazy things we did.

Setting off from Scotch Corner we headed up towards Gretna Green. Again, the road was pretty straight and so the slow speed wobble didn't bother us too much. Just south of Gretna we came up to a traffic jam. Now normally we would have weaved in and out of the lines of traffic and slowly progressed to the front. In fact, this is what we attempted to do. But there were two major problems. As we slowly passed between the stationary lines of cars the wobble made it very difficult to keep a straight course. Mick acted as a stabilizer by walking his hands along the roofs of the cars on either side, looking like he was paddling a two-wheel canoe down a river of traffic.

We were making good progress towards the front of the queue when we encountered our second problem. Some of the car drivers in front spotted us approaching in their rear-view mirrors. Now one of the great advantages of riding a motorcycle is the fact that you can negotiate traffic jams and get through much quicker. Unfortunately, some car drivers don't like this biker's perk. A few of the drivers ahead of us started to pull closer together and blocked our way. We were then stuck, sandwiched between two lines of traffic.

I can't understand the attitude of these obstructive drivers. Perhaps they are fed up with being stuck and resent the freedom of the bikers to keep moving. Whatever it is I'm glad not all car drivers have this attitude. Some even move over to allow more room for bikers to get past. If you are one these, please accept my heartfelt thanks and appreciation. Luckily the driver on the outside of us was one these kind individuals. As the traffic inched forward, he held back until there was space for us to get to the outside of the jam. We were then able to cruise down the outside of the queue and continue on our merry way. As we passed our "bike blockers" they started shouting in frustration and honking their horns. Mick saluted them in an appropriate way.

On reaching the Scottish border we both let out a cheer. You'd think that we'd escaped from a POW camp and had just crossed the Swiss frontier! Mick put on his posh British officer's voice. "Jolly good show Caruthers. We're home and dry old boy. Those blighters can't get us now. It's a home run."

We were still in high spirits as we entered the famous town of Gretna Green. Most of you will know that Gretna Green is famous as a destination for eloping couples. In the old days English law said you couldn't get married without your parents' consent if you were under the age of 21. Scottish law was different. You could get married at the age of 16 even without your parents' permission. Consequently, under-age English couples would secretly make the trek north and get hitched at the first town over the border – Gretna Green.

The first building happened to be the Blacksmith's, so this became the traditional venue for these romantic settings. Of course, things have changed over the years, but for some reason some couples still want their wedding ceremony to take place at the Smithy's Forge. There's money to be made in modern weddings so the tradition has developed into a lucrative business. It is also a popular tourist attraction, and souvenirs can be bought by the bucket full.

Now Mick and I were good friends, but we had no desire to get married. Neither did we want any souvenirs. After taking a quick look around we continued our journey.

Our trip wasn't carefully planned, and we had no specific itinerary, but my mum's cousin had recommended a place called Croy Bay, near to the town of Girvan on the west coast. He said there was a great camping site there that would welcome bikers. Taking his advice, we headed west and eventually reached the coast.

It was indeed a lovely place, so we quickly started searching for the camp site. It looked promising. The site was clearly sign posted and a tree lined avenue led to the gates of a professional and well-maintained site. After a hard day's riding we were both ready to set up the tent, stretch out and chill out.

No sooner had we dismounted when a woman burst out of reception and walked purposely towards us. She did not look welcoming.

"Yes; can I help you?" she said tersely.

I explained that we wanted to camp for the night and hoped that she could fit us in. I joked that we wouldn't take up too much space – just a motorcycle and a two-man tent.

Her face was like stone. "We don't cater for tents here. You better try somewhere else." She then turned and walked back towards reception.

We could see clearly that there were tents pitched on the site, so Mick decided to challenge her.

"Excuse me Mrs – we can see canvass dwellings all over the place. Where we come from, we call them tents."

The women froze in her steps and for a moment there was silence. Then she bawled, "Ralph, can you come out here. I think we've got trouble."

The next thing we saw was an enormous man, built like a brick outhouse, striding towards us. "What seems to be the problem lads" he said in a gruff baritone voice.

I then told him we simply wanted a pitch for the night, and we could see they did indeed have other tents dotted around.

"Ah," replied the man, "my wife obviously didn't explain clearly enough. We do have tents, but not your kind of tents,"

I was just about to describe our tent and explain that it was no different from most other tents, when three more men emerged from reception. They were younger and probably Ralph's sons. They were no more friendly than Ralph and his wife. Sour faces seemed to be a family trait.

All four men surrounded us, and Ralph pushed his face close to mine. "Let me make it clear young man," he said in a menacing, aggressive growl, "you are not welcome here; so clear off".

Now Mick never usually backed off from a confrontation (he'd got missing teeth to prove it), but even he could see we were hopelessly outnumbered. Discretion is the better part of valour. In other words – we knew we were licked. It was time to leave.

With dignity we mounted our trusty steed and rode off. Mick turned and saluted them in an appropriate way.

In those days bikers had to get used to prejudice. It's much more respectable to be a biker today. Middle-class, middle-aged men, riding super machines, costing more than a family car, and wearing hundreds of pounds worth of designer gear. In our day it was mainly working-class lads on affordable, often older bikes, wearing jeans and a scruffy leather jacket.

The newsreels of Rockers fighting Mods on Brighton beach didn't help the image of the poor Greaser on two wheels. A biker's leather jacket could get you refused service in a café, denied permission to camp, barred from pubs and Guest Houses and even picked on by the police.

Not feeling too downhearted, we looked for somewhere else to camp with a more friendly environment. We headed for the beach car park. The car park attendant was a very friendly Scotsman who quickly restored our faith in human nature. He explained that in that area camping had gone up market, and we were unlikely to find an established site willing to accept us even for one night.

He then winked and said, "If you drive along the beach towards those sand dunes you could camp there without anyone bothering you."

"What if someone in authority comes along? Won't they move us on?"

He touched the side of his nose and said, "On this beach, son, I am the one in authority."

In high spirits we set off along the sand. I was Steve McQueen riding along a sun-drenched California beach. Life didn't get much better than this.

Our good mood didn't last long. After driving through a rock pool, we hit a patch of deep sand and lost control. It was a soft landing and neither of us was hurt. We both laughed as we went to pick up the bike. My laughter did not last as I saw the state of my beloved machine.

It was covered in salt water and then to make it worse the sand had stuck to the moist surface. Two deadly enemies of anyone's pride and joy; sand and salt! Something snapped inside me. I was tired. I was hungry. I had been treated like dirt by the camp site owners; and now my bike was thoroughly messed up. I lost it completely. I started to shout. I started to swear. I kicked the sand and kicked the bike tyres. I was literally foaming at the mouth.

Mick had seen me lose my temper before, but never like this. He later told me that he thought I was having a nervous breakdown (although he called it a nervous bread van). Bless him, he just sat on the sand and waited for me to calm down. I know the sight of me upset him, but he had the sense to patiently wait until the storm had subsided and I fell exhausted on the sand. We sat in total silence for a good while. After about 10 minutes we both sensed it was time to get up. Still in silence we dusted ourselves down, cleaned the bike as best as we could, rearranged and secured the luggage and rode back slowly to the car park.

The kind attendant had seen from a distance what had happened, and he probably felt a bit responsible, but we reassured him that we were okay and said that we were sure to find somewhere else to camp. He wished us luck and we went despondently on our way.

Riding down the coastal road I was having serious doubts about ever finding a place to camp. Mick must have felt the same, but we kept our feelings to ourselves. It looked like we would have to wait until dark and pitch our tent anywhere that was out of sight. Just then I noticed something in the distance. It was hard to make out at first, but as we came closer, we saw it was a small group of tents pitched by the roadside. It was obviously not a recognised site, but merely a small patch of grass situated by the sea. Only a few rocks separated it from the waves.

We pulled to a halt and dismounted. We soon surmised it was a small group of family and friends who were unofficially camping by the sea. They all turned to face us. We scanned their faces looking for signs of welcome or rejection. I was the first to speak.

"I hope you don't mind me asking, but we're desperately trying to find somewhere to camp. Is there any chance of us joining you?"

They all seemed to react together, and their smiles said it was welcome not rejection. One young man spoke up on their behalf, "Aw man, we'd be glad to have you. There's just one space left and it's yours."

They all came to shake our hands, even the little kids, and we introduced ourselves. It seemed that they were a church group from Glasgow. They were not the type of Christians that we were used to. They too had been rejected from the posh camp site because they had arrived in an old furniture removal truck. We all laughed as we realised we were all in the same boat; segregated and ostracised.

They helped us erect our tent and asked if we were hungry. Oh boy, were we hungry. They pointed to a Calor gas stove on a flat rock by the sea. On it was a large pan like the ones they have in school canteens. In the pot meat and vegetables were cooking in a thick sauce, and it smelled delicious. A few minutes later we were tucking into a plate full of stew and soaking up the gravy with chunks of bread. What a meal.

It is strange that one moment you can be feeling so low, and then after meeting kind and welcoming people and sharing a meal followed by a hot mug of tea, you can be on the top of the world. These people didn't seem to have a lot of money or material possessions, but they certainly had something even more important. They were an excellent advert for their religion, and once more we were reminded of just how good people could be.

After letting the meal settle, Mick and I lay down in the tent and relaxed. We'd travelled about 300 miles and had a very interesting day. The bike was running well, despite the salt and sand, and we felt good. One thing more was needed to end a great day – a visit to a traditional Scottish pub. We asked our new friends if they knew of such a place, and they directed us to a hostelry just a mile away. We quickly stashed all our gear into the tent and set off for our night out. And what a night it was. The bike ran like a dream without the heavy luggage (this time with no slow speed wobbles}, and we soon arrived at our destination.

We stepped inside and encountered an idyllic scene. The place was packed with local people. We were the only strangers, but not for long. They soon warmed to us and accepted us like honorary Scots. They talked with us. Joked with us and laughed with us. Then, as if that wasn't good enough, the musicians arrived. No, it wasn't bagpipes (you can't have everything), but it was a fiddler accompanied by piano accordion and penny whistle. It may sound naff to modern kids, but we were in heaven. Traditional Scottish pub, local Scottish people, traditional Scottish music and Scottish beer (most of it paid for by our new Scottish friends.)

We left that place buzzing. We had had a genuine Caledonian experience – better than any tourist organisation could organise. Wow! We were ecstatic! Surely nothing could spoil this fantastic evening. Well almost nothing,

When I tried to kick-start the bike, the kick-start pedal didn't turn over the engine. I tried again thinking I must have inadvertently pulled the clutch lever. No, at the second attempt it was the same result. The kick-start just moved without turning the engine over. It was late, and I'd had a few drinks, so I couldn't really think straight. I decided if the kick-start didn't work, we could always bump start it. We put the bike in second gear, pushed it downhill, and then I jumped on and let out the clutch. Nothing. Even this didn't turn the engine over. Only one thing for it – we would have to push the bike back to the campsite.

By the time we reached the tent it was very dark, and we were very tired. Any repairs would have to wait until the morning. We slipped into our sleeping bags with heavy hearts. By this time the effects of the beer had worn off, and we were both worried about what tomorrow would bring.

Neither of us slept very well that night. I was trying to work out the best plan of action if I couldn't repair the bike. Perhaps I could persuade our Christian hosts to transport the bike to Glasgow station and put it on a train back to Chesterfield. I knew they were likely to agree to this because of their obvious Christian charity, but I was reluctant to take advantage of them and intrude on their holiday.

In the darkness I decided there was another option. I decided to pray. At first, I thought I'd try a Biblical miracle prayer – "Lord, by Thy mighty hand touch this unworthy machine and cause it to regain its usefulness." On second thought I came up with a prayer that I felt more comfortable with – "Lord, you know we're in trouble. Please help me to diagnose the problem and give me the skill to repair it. Amen." I then finally fell asleep.

There is an old saying – "They are so heavenly minded that they are no earthly use." God sometimes wants us to be practical in our faith. I remember hearing a missionary give a talk about his work in the far north of Canada. His name was Marshall, and he was a big strong man dressed in a lumberjack shirt. His name and appearance both appealed to me as a young boy. He related how he had prayed for several days that God would fix his faulty hurricane lamp. The lamp continued to flicker and splutter. He eventually took the lamp down and had a good look at it. The lamp didn't need a miracle; it needed a good cleaning.

God can use our skills and talents. We can't be lazy and expect God to fix all our problems, but we can expect God to help and guide us as we get on with job.

We didn't need an alarm clock to wake us in the morning. The kids on the site were up at 7am and making enough noise to waken the dead. Before rising Mick and I discussed our problem. Mick was in no way religious, so I was a bit embarrassed to tell him about my prayer. To my amazement he told me I wasn't the only one praying. He too had made a request to God.

"What did you pray for?" I asked.

He replied in a serious tone, "I asked that you would discover what was the problem and then repair it. So, you better get on with it," "No pressure then." I replied.

On emerging from the tent, we were greeted with a hot mug of tea, a thick slice of bread, and told to toast it over the stove. The fresh toast was then smothered with butter and jam. After finishing this simple, but delicious breakfast I got on with the job in hand.

I laid my limited assortment of tools on the ground next to the bike. In the cold light of day, I knew what the problem was. The clutch wasn't doing its job, but I knew it wasn't just as simple as adjusting it. I had a feeling the clutch assembly was spinning on its tapered shaft and so I had to take off the crank case cover and have a proper look.

As I started the job an audience gathered around me, all pretending to be experts and give me advice. The sun was shining, and the good-natured banter spurred me on.

I removed the crank case cover, and it was just as I thought. The clutch centre had come loose. I told Mick that the "tab washer" had broken, and his response was, "Well that's okay, you don't clean your ears anyway." This got a laugh from "the audience", and the whole thing had turned into a social event.

The large hexagon nut on the clutch centre had to be loosened, but none of my usual spanners were big enough. I was stuck. Mick picked up the spark plug spanner and suggested it might fit. Arrogantly I dismissed his suggestion, but the crowd backed Mick and persuaded me to at least give it a try. To my embarrassment it fitted perfectly.

After removing the clutch centre, I found that the woodruff key had sheared in half and the tapered shaft was scored and scratched. Of course, I didn't have a replacement woodruff key or tab washer. I decided to re-fit the clutch centre and tighten it so tight that even without the woodruff key it couldn't spin on the tapered shaft. Thank goodness the spark plug spanner had a decent handle on it and I was able to tighten the nut super tight. I even used my foot to provide extra pressure.

After replacing the cover and re-fitting the kick-start, it was time to give it a try. The engine started second kick, as always, and we all let out a loud cheer. I gave the bike a quick run down the road, and it worked perfectly. That interim repair lasted for the remainder of the road trip (over 800 miles). On reaching home I finally did the job properly and replaced the tab washer and woodruff key.

Our hosts wanted us to stay for another day, but we wanted to be on the road again as soon as possible. We took down the tent and stowed it neatly with all the other luggage on the rear carrier. We were doing our final check, when the leader of the group came across to us, looking quite serious. He looked me in the eye and asked me, straight out, "John are you a Christian?"

I was quite taken aback by the question. I wanted to give the simple answer "no", and get away as quickly as I could, but then I looked at Mick. He knew my secret. He knew that my parents were Christians. He knew as a child I had regularly attended Sunday School. He knew I still went to church most Sundays. He knew I had a good knowledge of the Bible. He knew that I believed in my head everything that a Christian should believe. He would find it very puzzling if I now denied my religion.

I thought for a moment and then replied, "I suppose I am a Christian, but I'm not a very good one." I was thinking of my temper tantrum the day before; my drinking and smoking; my swearing and the dirty jokes. Jesus said, "By their fruit you shall know them". The fruit I produced was hardly Christian.

This simple man of God put his hand on my shoulder and told me something astounding. "Last evening when you were both at the pub, we held a prayer meeting. The Lord revealed to us that you had a Christian background and that you were trying to run away from it. John, God has a very special plan for your life and can use you greatly in His service. You are trying to run away from Him, but He is your loving Father and is waiting patiently for you to come home."

I was really moved by his words. Even Mick felt something special had happened. The man then called the rest of the group to gather round us. They prayed that God would keep us safe and give us a good journey. They even prayed for the bike to run well for the rest of the trip.

After an emotional farewell we set off on the next part of our adventure. Mick turned and waved to them. He did not give them an inappropriate salute.

❉

Chapter Two

Mick and I didn't talk much when we were on the road. This was before the days of Bluetooth and earpieces etc., and what with the sound of the engine and the air rushing past, holding a conversation was quite difficult. A crash helmet covering your ears didn't help the situation. If Mick needed to communicate, he would tap my helmet and shout a short message. If I wished to speak to him, I would tap his leg, turn my head to one side and holler my sentence or two. As a consequence, we spent most of the time watching the road or scenery without uttering a word. This is good for the soul. It gives you plenty of time to think. It also helps you appreciate your surroundings.

A journey by motorcycle is fundamentally different from a journey in a car. In an enclosed vehicle you are watching the landscape, rather like watching the TV. You're encased in a bubble – warm and cosy and sheltered from the elements. You chat with your friend and can even ignore the most beautiful scenery. You see the landscape, but you don't feel it.

On a bike you are truly part of the landscape. You feel the heat or cold. You feel the rain. You feel the air rushing past. You even smell the smells. Of course, when the weather is bad, it's not so enjoyable. You have to take the rough with the smooth, but whatever the conditions you still feel very much alive and in touch with nature.

I was doing a lot of thinking on this trip and being on the bike in lovely scenery was having a spiritual affect. I thought about the man's words back at the roadside camp. Perhaps I was trying to run away from God. Perhaps I was like Jonah in the Bible, trying to travel in the opposite direction to God's will. I was grateful that, unlike Jonah, I was in Scotland and not inside Wales!

I thought about those lovely Christian people on that tiny patch of grass next to the rocks and sea. It wasn't the most luxurious holiday, but they seemed so happy and contented. Maybe they had something that we all need. A simple lifestyle and a simple faith. I was a bit like my over-loaded motorcycle – too much junk on my back, wobbling along life's road and finding it hard to hold a straight line. Wow, even the bike was getting spiritual.

The broken tab washer and the sheared woodruff key also had a spiritual message for me. They should have been replaced the last time I dismantled the clutch, but I couldn't be bothered ordering the parts. The manual said they should be replaced but I knew better. They were little things, but very important. There were little things in my life that needed sorting out, but I couldn't be bothered. I just piled on the junk and carried on regardless. Maybe I was heading for a breakdown.

I was still deep in thought when Mick tapped my helmet and shouted, "I'm dying for a leak!"

Well, from the sublime to the mundane. I pulled into the next layby and Mick went for a short walk among the trees. I took the opportunity to check the bike over. The petrol tank was still half full. The engine didn't seem to be over-heating and the oil level was fine. I took a leak myself, stretched my legs and massaged my booty. The bike started second kick, as always, and we were on the road again.

After a while we both noticed a change in the landscape. Gradually the number of buildings increased, and the roads became more congested. We realised we were getting near to Glasgow, the first city on our route.

My method of getting through a city was both simple and naïve. I just headed for the centre and tried to head out the opposite end. I'd used this method to get through London and it had served me well. On that occasion I rode past famous sites like Big Ben and the Houses of Parliament and had some informative chats with several taxi drivers along the way. Being on a bike makes it easy to ask for directions and easy to turn around if you go wrong. On that occasion I just kept asking, "Which way to The Thames mate?" Then after crossing the mighty river, I just headed south looking for signs to Brighton. Who needs sat nav?

The signs for Glasgow's centre were very clear and we were soon in the heart of the city. In recent years Glasgow has gained renown as a city of culture, but it didn't seem very "cultural" to us. Some areas appeared run-down and a bit rough. On one street there was a man lying sprawled on the pavement. He wasn't moving, so we assumed he was either dead or dead-drunk. Whichever it was, we were amazed to see people casually walking round him. Some even stepped over him as they carried on with their conversations. Mick and I both let out laughs of disbelief. We had never seen anything like this total disregard for a fellow human being. He might as well had been a bin bag full of rubbish.

It was a great relief to leave the city and we were soon out on the country roads again heading for Loch Lomond. Heading up through the Trossachs, the countryside was beautiful, and the sun was still shining. It was such a contrast to the city we had left behind. The air felt clean and healthy and once more we were on cloud nine. We found a campsite in a place called Luss, right on the shores of the loch. In fact, we pitched our tent just a few yards away from its crystal water. I can't begin to tell you how good it felt.

We had now clocked up 400 miles and we were ready for a bit of rest and recuperation.

The first thing we did was have a swim in the loch. It was cold, but very refreshing. Mick commented that it was cold round The Trossachs, and I had to agree. We soon dried off, dressed, and set off for the nearest pub. We wanted a cold pint and a hot meal.

On our way to the pub, I was shocked to see a man and his son walking towards us. I couldn't believe my eyes. He was a well-known preacher from my hometown. His name was Ken Hartley, and he regularly preached at our church. He was a really nice bloke. His mop of blonde hair and his handsome face gave him the appearance of an angel. I greatly respected this man and normally I would have greeted him and had a good chat. But there I was in my leather jacket, smoking a cigarette and wanting to be the teenage rebel. I'm ashamed to say I pretended not to see him and quickly ducked inside the pub. I wasn't sure if he'd seen me.

Mick asked me what was going on. I replied, "Oh nothing. I thought for a minute that I knew that bloke."

Mick let it pass, but I knew he was puzzled by my furtive behaviour. I brushed it off and said, "Come on, let's get something to eat. I'm starving."

It was years later that I confessed to Ken how I had ignored him and his son at Loch Lomond. He then informed me that he had indeed spotted me coming towards him and expected to receive a friendly greeting like, "Hi Ken - Fancy seeing you here". He was shocked and disappointed to see me dart off and realised that I was purposely trying to avoid him. Instead of being indignant and slagging me off for smoking and being anti-social, he and his son had then driven back to their caravan and prayed for me. They didn't care about the leather jacket image, or the drinking and smoking. They liked me! They asked God to protect me and bless me. Oh, if only more Christians could be like them.

Because of this shameless snubbing of Ken, poetic justice should have decreed that the rest of my evening would be a disaster, but this wasn't the case. Mick and I had a tasty fish and chip supper and then retired to the bar. There we met two middle aged couples and had a brilliant time socialising with them. Mick was in his element reeling out his amusing anecdotes and being an all-round entertainer. I'd heard most of his funny stories before, but these people had had a few drinks and loved him. When it was time to leave, one of the ladies offered to give us breakfast in the morning. Of course, we accepted the offer.

Walking back to the tent we were in a happy mood. Perhaps the beer had had its effect, but it wasn't just the alcohol. The food had been good; the company had been good, and the scenery was idyllic. We sat at the entrance to the tent and looked out across the beautiful loch. The moon was shining on the water, and we could see the black silhouettes of the mountains on the far shore. We sat in silence, taking it all in. Then the light show began. Lightning began to flash in the distance like some natural laser show. There was no sound of thunder, but the illuminations were truly sensational. After watching this phenomenon for half an hour, we crawled into our sleeping bags and quickly fell asleep.

It must have been about 2am when the crash of thunder disturbed my slumber. The storm had finally caught up with us. I had never heard such loud rolls of thunder. It seemed to shake the ground. I peered at Mick through the darkness, and he was still sleeping like a baby.

Then the rain started. Torrential rain. It felt like the tent was under a waterfall. Mick continued to sleep through it. He must have had more drink than me. He was comatose. I know Boy

Scouts dig drainage ditches around their tents, but we were not Boy Scouts. We were Not Prepared! Reaching out from the sleeping bag, I could feel that the ground sheet was rippling. A small river was flowing underneath us. Mick slept on, and knowing I could do nothing about it, I drew my arm back into the sleeping bag and rejoined Mick in the land of nod.

The sun was shining when we eventually woke up. My first words were, "Mick did you hear anything last night?"

He looked puzzled and replied. "Hear anything? Like what?"

"Like the loudest thunder you have ever heard. Like the sound of a waterfall on the tent."

He laughed and confessed he hadn't heard anything. He had slept right through it all. He then suddenly stopped laughing and cried out, "Oh no! I think I've wet myself!"

He quickly struggled out of his wet sleeping bag fearing the worst. It took him a couple of minutes to realise that the moisture was a result of rainwater rather than urine. We then put on our damp clothes and promptly emptied the soggy contents of the tent out onto the grass. We hoped the sun would soon dry things out.

We hung the damp sleeping bags on a nearby tree and then spread out the rest of our stuff. We couldn't believe this large collection of kit had actually fitted on the back of the bike.

Sitting at the side of the tent, we felt rather damp and depressed. It seems stupid now, but we hadn't really planned for wet weather. There is an old saying, "There's no such thing as bad weather; just inappropriate clothing." Well, our clothing was inappropriate! In the bar the previous night one Scottish sage had sensed that a storm was on its way. He had commented, rather smugly, "I hope you've brought your packer-macs you sassenachs?"

Naively we hadn't got a packer-mac or any other kind of waterproofs, and we were now feeling rather low and foolishly ill-prepared. Our low mood was soon lifted by the arrival of our breakfast. The lady from the night before had been true to her word and was walking towards us with a large silver tray. On it was laid out two boiled eggs in posh egg cups, buttered toast "soldiers", bone-china cups, saucers and milk jug, and an enormous pot of tea covered by a bright knitted tea cosy. It looked like something that the butler would serve up for two young lords, instead of two scruffy bikers.

We thanked the lady profusely and tucked into the feast. When the boiled eggs had quickly disappeared, she re-appeared carrying two croissants with butter and jam. We had never seen croissants before, but we soon learned what to do with them. Needless to say, there were no leftovers, when we returned the tray and crockery to her caravan.

Once again, we were amazed just how kind and generous people could be. We were also amazed, once again, how a delicious meal can lift your spirits. We could now face anything!

The first thing we had to face was a quick ride to the nearby town of Alexandria. Mick had torn his jeans on the first day of the trip, and the tear was getting bigger by the hour. He was a natural exhibitionist, but even he couldn't stand this kind of exposure. Rips in jeans are fashionable these days, but not in the places Mick had them. He had spent the previous night in the pub either sitting down or standing with his back to the bar. He was desperate to purchase some new jeans. We soon found a small clothes shop, bought the jeans, and we were back at the campsite in no time.

We spent the rest of the afternoon reading the paperbacks that we'd taken with us. I remember my book was an adventure story set in the Highlands of Scotland. How appropriate.

After finishing the short novel, I decided to give the bike a good looking over. I first checked the dipstick and found the oil level was quite low. I always carried a small can of oil with me, and I emptied its contents into the engine, making a mental note to buy some more at the next petrol station. Removing the spark plug I found it was a bit sooty. This meant that the petrol/air mixture was a bit rich, but I wasn't going to mess about trying to tune the carburettor. The engine was running well and that was good enough for me. The tyres were the right pressure for the weight we were carrying, and the lights and horn showed that the battery was in fine shape. It looked as if the old girl was in the best of health. I laughed at myself when I realised how my attitude to my bike had changed. I now genuinely cared for the machine and my maintenance had taken on a new quality. This hadn't always been the case.

I got my first motorcycle when I was 17. My dad bought it off a bloke at work for the princely sum of £5. It was a Honda 90 C200 and seemed in pretty good condition. It started first kick and ticked over nicely. My dad and I couldn't understand why it was so cheap. I couldn't wait to ride it, so I got the insurance and tax sorted out, borrowed a helmet and within a few a few days I was on the road. It was only then that I realised why it only cost a fiver.

Honda 90 C200

The engine idled nicely, but when you opened up the throttle it just groaned and lost power. I was devastated and thought we'd made a big mistake. The cheating man had sold us a dud! Dad wasn't so pessimistic. He suspected that the carburettor wasn't getting enough air and thought that the choke might be stuck on. He then removed the side panel to inspect the air filter. It looked filthy so he took it out and told me to try riding the bike without it. To my joy it went like a rocket (well a 90cc rocket). I had had my first lesson in motorcycle maintenance. Engines need a good supply of air. They also need a good spark and petrol.

It was too late to buy a new air filter, so my dad made a few holes in it with a screwdriver and wrapped it with the leg of an old pair of mum's tights.

"That should work for the time being," he said, "but get that air filter replaced as soon as possible."

He also told me to regularly check the oil level. "A bike is like a human being. It needs air; it needs food (petrol), and it needs oil. Oil is like blood to a bike. Running out of food won't kill you, but running out of blood is always fatal. An engine can survive running out of petrol, but if it runs out of oil it seizes up and dies. Everything locks up as if rigor mortis has set in."

I thought he'd explained things really well, but to quote the Bible, "They have ears but do not listen." I didn't take him seriously. That air filter never got replaced, and I never checked the oil level. My dad was a gifted engineer, and I must have been a big disappointment to him. I would strip the threads on nuts, bolts and studs. I'd break delicate parts of any machine. He would watch me in exasperation as I seemed to go on wrecking sprees.

"Why do you have to be so ham-fisted?" he would groan. "Use a bit of finesse! Use a bit of finesse!"

It all came to a head when the bike actually did seize up. I had to push it home and it was after midnight when I got in. Dad was asleep in bed, but my noisy entrance woke him up.

"Is that you John?" he called from the bedroom. "I didn't hear the bike."

"No dad," I said sheepishly, "I had to push it home. I think the engine's seized."

On hearing this he got straight out of bed and went outside in his pyjamas and slippers. He checked that the engine was truly solid and then shone his torch on the dipstick. There wasn't one drop of oil on it.

"It's seized alright," he said in despair. "I told you to check the oil! Why didn't you check the oil?"

My reply was pitiful. "Sorry dad, I forgot."

"Forgot my arse!" was his disgusted response. He then went back to bed.

That was the first and only time I had heard my father come close to using bad language. It was a wake-up call. From that time on I decided to get my act together. I wanted him to be proud of me, and in the years that followed I'm sure he was.

By now we were both hungry and so decided to pay the pub another visit. This time we ordered a traditional roast dinner after which we took our places at the bar. The middle-aged people we had met the previous night were deep in conversation with another couple, so we moved to another part of the pub where a large group of young people were gathered. It was a like a small branch of The United Nations. There were Americans, Canadians, French, Scandinavians and four lovely girls from Ireland. There may have been more nationalities. We lost count.

Up until then we had thought we were the great adventurers, travelling hundreds of miles, but these guys put us to shame. Some of them had travelled thousands of miles and were planning to travel thousands more before they returned home. We found it fascinating to listen to their different accents and hear their individual stories. They in turn found us quite quaint. They thought that all English people spoke like David Niven, and they were so amused to hear our Derbyshire accents. It made us both realise how people from various nations could get along ok, at least for one evening. I was amazed to discover that one of the Irish girls was going to attend the same college as myself, and we made arrangements to meet up at the start of term.

It was very late when "The International Brigade" disbanded. We said an emotional farewell and returned to our tent. Our "sun-dried" sleeping bags felt nice and cosy. Fortunately, there was no thunder or rain in the night to disturb our sleep. We were awakened by a gentle female voice informing us that she had brought us breakfast. We opened the tent, and the kind lady handed us bacon rolls and mugs of hot tea. Wow! Breakfast in bed! (or was it breakfast in bag?)

We were genuinely beginning to believe that the world was a wonderful place, and that all people could live together in harmony and peace. If only.

After this delicious breakfast we were soon packed up and ready to ride. Our new friends waved us off as we rode out of the campsite. As we left, we sang a line from the Canned Heat song, "On the Road Again". This became the setting off ritual for the rest of the trip.

Chapter 3

From Luss we set off directly north on the A82. The road ran along the water's edge for the entire length of Loch Lomond. It was truly a fantastic experience. Sunshine, water, and mountains. The stuff of dreams for any biker.

We eventually left the loch behind us and continued on the A82 for another 35 miles to Glen Coe. We stopped here to visit the Glen Coe Monument. It commemorates the Massacre of Glen Coe, which took place on 13 February 1692.

An estimated 30 members of the Clan MacDonald were killed by Scottish government forces, although inter-clan rivalry may have also been involved.

It seemed strange that such a scenic place should be infamous for mass murder. We spent a few moments in silence, contemplating the awful history of this beautiful Glen. We both realised that such massacres had taken place throughout time, and even in our own lifetime such atrocities were not unknown.

We were soon "On the Road Again" and this time heading for Fort William, a name that conjured up ideas of a John Wayne western film. We hoped we could get there safely without being attacked by the fierce natives. In our minds, we were modern day cowboys riding The Highlands.

We were a little disappointed that Fort William was not surrounded by a pine-log stockade fence, but we were relieved to get there and find somewhere to eat. Our initial intention was to find a campsite at Fort William, but we had made good time and there was plenty of daylight left. After a quick meal we decided to press on to our next destination – Loch Ness. It was only 50 miles away, and we would be there before our buttocks could give us any trouble. We didn't need a map. We had been on the A82 all day and would stay on this stretch of tarmac all the way to Inverness.

It was rugged terrain. During the Second World War, the commandos had used this area as a training ground. At a place called Spean Bridge there is a monument to these brave men. We thought we were roughing it, but our trip was like a Sunday School Outing compared to their extreme training. It always surprises me why men would volunteer for such an arduous life.

Commando Memorial

Their missions were sometimes suicidal, and they suffered all sorts of deprivations. Hey; it takes all types! We were just grateful for men like these who were willing to give their all to protect us from such evil enemies as the Nazis.

From Spean Bridge we rode along the shores of Loch Lochy and took in the majestic scenery. Normal people start to feel rather spiritual when they are confronted by beautiful landscapes. It's only in modern times that scientists have explained how we got mountains, valleys and lakes etc. Glaciers gouged out great troughs. Volcanoes erupted and became mountains. Rivers eroded the rocks and made caves and gorges. Yes, they give us the scientific facts, but they can't explain the way we feel when we survey the beauties of our natural world. These sights generate feelings of awe and wonder that go beyond science. A sunset is just the sun's rays passing through layers of atmosphere that create different hues of red and orange. A rainbow is just light being refracted through rain drops and splitting into the colours of the spectrum. Why should these scientific phenomena generate such feelings.

Primitive man could see the hand of the gods in such panoramas of majesty. High places became Holy places. Man is basically religious and wants to worship. He looks at the stars and senses something beyond them. Twenty First Century man dismisses this and has a pragmatic attitude. We don't need a God anymore. We've worked it all out mathematically. We know all the answers without any divine intervention. Yes, we know how everything came into being. But we don't know why! We are left with an empty feeling of meaningless existence. As the Scottish play says, "Life's but a walking shadow; a poor player, that struts and frets his hour upon the stage, and then is heard no more: it is a tale told by an idiot, full of sound and fury, signifying nothing."

My life was full of sound and fury, full of youthful energy, but just whizzing around in all directions and heading nowhere. To quote Mick, "I'm just a stray bullet, ricocheting from one experience to another. There is no plan."

The Bible makes it clear that there is more to life than scientific facts, but it says we can recognise spiritual facts through witnessing physical entities. In Romans chapter 1:20 it even says that we can use visible facts to verify God's existence. "For since the creation of the world God's invisible qualities - his eternal power and divine nature – have been clearly seen, being understood from what has been made."

The famous Christian Preacher, Charles Haddon Spurgeon, said that if you wanted to study God there were two important books you should read. To establish God's existence, you should read the book of Nature (Creation). If you want to get to know God intimately you should read the Bible.

I was deep in thought, contemplating all this, when suddenly I saw a car coming round the bend and heading straight for us. The large Mercedes, with German number plates, was on the wrong side of the road and was sure to hit us head on. I quickly turned the handlebars and avoided total disaster. I remember gliding past the side of the car and leaving the road. All I could hear was the air rushing by. Everything seemed to happen in slow motion.

Suddenly we were back in real time. I was heading for a rock, and in panic I slammed on both brakes. Unfortunately, we were now on roadside gravel and the bike slid from under us. Mick was thrown clear, but I was still holding on to the handlebars, and as the bike slid to a halt, I was stuck with my right leg pinned to the ground. I was relieved to feel no pain, but I couldn't move. It was then that I noticed petrol dripping onto my jeans. The engine was very hot, and I could feel the heat of it on my leg. I could see and smell the petrol on my jeans. It was then that I went into total panic. I had visions of me and the bike turning into a fireball.

"Mick! Mick! Get the bike off my leg. Get the bike off my leg!"

Mick rushed across. He lifted the bike to free my leg and I quickly rolled away from the danger.

The man from the Mercedes had stopped a little further down the road and came running back to us. He was obviously shaken (but not as shaken as me). In a very strong German accent, he began to apologise profusely for causing the accident. It was clear what had happened. He had been travelling on the empty road and inadvertently reverted to driving on the right-hand side. It was only when he met us coming the opposite way that he realised the error of his ways. Fortunately, he had jerked his steering wheel at the same time as I jerked the handlebars, thus averting tragic consequences.

His wife then joined him and was in floods of tears. She kept asking us if we were hurt, and repeatedly said, "Mein Gott! Mein Gott!" which we presumed meant "my God". We assured them that we were not seriously injured, with just a few bumps and scratches. Luckily, by the time we hit the dirt (gravel) we were going quite slow.

We then checked the bike over. There was surprisingly very little damage. The luggage and my leg had prevented most of the bike from hitting the ground. The rubber knob on the end of the footrest was hanging off. The brake lever had been rotated on the handlebars, but not broken, and one of the stays had broken off the front mudguard. That's all the damage we could find for the moment. The German wanted to exchange insurance details, but we declined to do this. His car had no damage at all, and our limited damage didn't warrant all the trouble of making a claim.

Besides this, my documents were at home, hundreds of miles away.

We told him that no real harm had been done and said that he should continue his journey and forget the unfortunate incident. In addition to this he was asked to promise to stay on the correct side of the road in future! He readily agreed to this, but seemed adamant that he should make some recompense. He produced £30 from his wallet and forced it into my hand. Before I could object too much, he and his wife had returned to their car and driven away. This time keeping to the left.

Mick and I started to laugh. We were so relieved to be unharmed and the laughter seemed to release all the stress of the crash. I found it amusing that my dad had survived the Germans bombing his street, and over 30 years later another German had almost killed his son! This time, however, there was no malice involved. The man and woman's concern for us had been moving, and his generosity was much appreciated; £30 was a fortune to us.

In twenty minutes, the damage to the bike had been sorted. I broke off the rubber end of the footrest, loosened the nut on the brake lever, re-positioned and re-tightened it. The repair of the mudguard stay was more of a problem. It had been rivetted to the mudguard and the rivet had been torn out, leaving a hole. Thank goodness for bendy, metal wire. I always carried a length of this with me. It came in handy for ad hoc roadside repairs. I simply coiled the wire tightly around the top of the stay and then threaded the other end of the wire through the rivet hole a couple of times, before twisting it tight with a pair of pliers. This repair lasted for the rest of the trip.

We were soon on our way again and managed to reach Loch Ness by the end of the afternoon. The campsite was at a place called Invermoriston. Our pitch was next to the loch but sadly there was a line of trees blocking our view. We had hoped to do a bit of Nessy watching from the comfort of our tent, but this was not to be.

We noticed that our fellow campers were not quite as friendly as the Loch Lomond crew. There were no offers of meals, and it was hard to start any kind of conversation. Perhaps it was another case of prejudice against bikers. Whatever it was we were glad to be on the site, and we quickly took a walk to the local pub for something to eat. Every cloud has a silvery lining, and our crash that day had financed the camping fees and a meal, with £15 left over for another day.

We stayed at the pub a couple of hours and then walked to a viewing point on the side of the loch. We both knew the Loch Ness monster story was a myth, but it was still exciting to look out across the water and imagine the monster's head appearing from the deep. Whether it was the temperature of the water, or the thought of the monster, we both refrained from swimming during our short stay.

Reconstruction of Nessie as a plesiosaur outside the Museum of Nessie[1]

---

[1] Photograph by Starablazkova is licensed under the creative commons attribution-share alike 3.0 unported license.

The next morning, we rose early and took advantage of the facilities of the campsite. The showers and toilets were very clean and well maintained, and we both felt like new men when we returned to the tent. We had a drink of water from the outside tap, and then loaded our gear on the bike. The lack of social interaction with our fellow campers encouraged us to move out early, and anyway, we enjoyed being on the road.

Before leaving Invermoriston, we visited the picturesque waterfall. Some tourists may miss this attraction because it's a five-minute walk from the car park. It's not the highest waterfall in the area, but the combination of large boulders and rapids make it well worth a visit. There is a beautiful bridge spanning the falls which was built by Thomas Telford in 1813. A new bridge replaced this in 1930, and now the old bridge is a superb vantage point to observe the torrents of water without worrying about passing traffic. Another visitor informed us that it was a great spot to watch the salmon leaping upstream. We assumed it wasn't salmon season, for we didn't catch sight of any during our short visit.

Invermoriston Old Bridge

After returning to the car park, we were soon "On the Road Again" and heading towards Inverness. It was a journey of only 30 miles, but we decided to stop there and grab something to eat. We found a roadside café and ordered a full English breakfast.

The man behind the counter informed us that he didn't do a full English, so we asked him what he recommended instead. He suggested fried egg and bacon, fried bread, beans and tomatoes.

"Isn't that the same as a full English breakfast?" Mick asked.

"Listen laddie," the man replied. "You're in Scotland now. That's what we call a Full Scottish Breakfast."

We thought he was splitting hairs, but whatever it was called it tasted delicious. After a hot mug of tea, we headed south on the A9. That day we intended riding all the way to Edinburgh. It was just over 150 miles (3 bum rests), but we had made an early start and knew we could make it easily. After the city of Perth, the A9 transformed into the M90 and headed almost directly south, past Kinross and then onto Edinburgh.

The last part of the journey was a little boring. Mile after mile of motorway, but at least we were burning up the miles, and no one was heading towards us on the wrong side of the road.

Here might be a good time to give a little praise to our Trusty Steed. People nowadays go touring Scotland on big BMW enduro bikes, or Honda Gold wings etc., and may think it's so easy. They don't usually break down and if they do they send for the AA. The powerful engines can cope with most hills without changing gear, and they gobble up the miles with ease. That's not the case with a 1965 Royal Enfield Crusader Sports. It has a single cylinder 250cc engine, and a top speed of 70mph (downhill with a tail wind). It's a very simple machine but it did a magnificent job. Remember it was carrying 2 adults and luggage for hundreds of miles and yet it's small engine never missed a beat. We really put it to the test, and it was not found wanting. I loved that bike, and the only time it broke down was entirely my fault. Shoddy Maintenance. It may not seem much to modern bikers, but I'm very proud of that journey. It may have used up a few pints oil, but as my dad said, "At least when you keep topping it up, the oil is always relatively new and clean. You are in fact constantly doing an oil change!"

Anyway, that's enough praise for the old girl. I said that the last part of the journey was boring, but there was an exception ie. Crossing the Firth of Forth Road Bridge.

The bridge itself is a beautiful piece of civil engineering. The road is suspended by giant cables that make impressive arcs. The road itself seems to be floating in mid-air. Crossing it on a motorcycle is fantastic. The wind, the smell of the sea, the smooth road surface; it's almost like flying. You feel so small compared to this massive structure. It's something I will remember all my life.

I thought of the film Easy Rider. One scene shows them crossing a bridge, but it was nowhere near as beautiful as this highway sculpture. In the film Peter Fonda and Dennis Hopper were riding customised Harley Davidsons, chrome plated and skilfully painted. Our little bike was nothing like their machines, but we were experiencing the same feelings of freedom and ecstasy.

That film had a real effect on my life. I was at an impressable age, and I soaked it in like a sponge. These two young men, crossing America on superb bikes was the stuff of dreams. I tried to emulate them in my own way. A few weeks before the Scottish trip I had set out on my own Easy Rider adventure. The imitation was almost comical. Instead of the highways of America, my journey took me through Wales. I took nothing with me.

Aping Peter Fonda, I had even thrown my watch on the kitchen table and said, "I won't be needing that."

My dad had laughed and said, "You'll regret that son". Of course, I didn't take any notice.

I picked up a Hippie who was hitch hiking, just like in the movie, and we both headed for a place called Abersoch, where his mother had a caravan. So far so good. I was following the script. However, when we reached our destination, he met some of his rich friends and dropped me like a brick. He was in fact not an authentic Hippie. His hair and clothes were right for the part, but he didn't have any brotherly love for me, and I was left friendless with nowhere to lay my weary head.

I headed out of town as darkness was falling. By this stage I wasn't enjoying the trip so much and was a bit nervous about sleeping rough in the open air. I stopped the bike by a gateway that led into a field. Opening the gate, I pushed the bike into the field, closed the gate behind me and spread my thin blanket on the ground. I'm embarrassed to say that as soon as I switched off the headlight I was filled with fear. I had never known total darkness before. No moon. No street lights. No houses. Just pitch darkness. I quickly rolled up the blanket and tied it on the bike. What a relief to kick up the engine and switch on the headlight. I was out of there like a shot and heading for the town of Caernarfon.

Nearing the outskirts of the town I found a petrol station that looked like it was open, but on further inspection it was only a self-service place. The petrol pump had a special cash tray. You had to insert an old-style pound note into this tray and then it would dispense a pound's worth of fuel. That doesn't seem much, but in those days £1 got me about 3 gallons of fuel. The forecourt was well lit, so I decided to check the oil. I pulled out the dip stick and found to my horror that the level was extremely low. The petrol tank was full but bitter experience told me I couldn't continue my journey without oil. I rode very slowly into town and found a car park near the waterfront.

Wrapping my blanket around me I curled up behind the car park attendant's wooden hut and tried to sleep. The place was reasonably well lit, but I still felt a little insecure sleeping alone under the stars. Eventually I dozed off. I don't know how long I slept but I was rudely awakened by a cat walking over my face. This really gave me a start. I sat bolt upright, and almost scared the cat to death. It let out a screech and sped off into the night.

After that I could sleep no more. I had no idea what time it was. I did sincerely regret not taking my watch. Heading down to the shore, I looked around to see if there were any signs of life. There was only one building with a light on, so I headed for it. Knocking gingerly on the door, I heard someone call "Come in". Entering the building I discovered it was a bakery. The baker asked me what I wanted, and I asked him the time. He looked at his watch and informed me it was four o'clock in the morning. I had at least four more hours before the petrol station opened. Four lonely, chilly, miserable hours.

At 6am the newsagent opened, and I bought the biggest newspaper on the shelf. I didn't read a word of it. Using it as insulation, I lined my leather jacket with it and took a nap. At last, the garage opened. I bought the oil and gave the bike a well-deserved "Blood Transfusion". Then I was on my way. Stopping for breakfast at the beautiful Swallow Falls I then headed for home as fast as my little wheels could take me. My Easy Rider adventure was over. It had lasted less than 24 hours. I vowed that I would never travel again without basic equipment. These basics included a tent, a sleeping bag, a can of oil, and course a watch.

Near the end of the Easy Rider film Billy says, "Hey man we've really made it. We're rich man. We can retire to Florida."

Wyatt gets all moody and claims they "blew it." Wyatt recognised they had failed to find the real freedom and spiritual fulfilment they were looking for.

I felt the same. That trip to Wales was a bit of a disaster, but it taught me quite a few lessons. The biggest lesson was that life is not always like a feature film. My daft, romantic ideas about freedom etc. had been challenged big time. I started thinking seriously about where my life was heading. Fact is different to fiction, and I had to sort my act out.

Now, let's get back to the Scottish trip. I used the same tactic to get through Edinburgh as I did in Glasgow. I headed for the city centre and soon arrived at a junction with the famous Princes Street. There was a line of traffic waiting at the junction, and we slowly went down the outside of it and took our place next to the leading car. A lone policeman was directing the traffic, and our eyes were fixed on him, waiting for him to wave us out. We knew that we had to be quick setting off, or the car next to us may cut us up. I was revving the bike like mad, and ready to let out the clutch at the first sign.

Both Mick and I thought the policeman had signalled us to move. I let the clutch out a little too fast and the bike did a wheelie for the first time in its life. The excess weight on the back was the reason for this unintentional stunt, and consequently we were heading straight for the startled policeman on one wheel. Fortunately, this bike was not designed for such maneuverers, and as I cut the revs the front wheel soon touched the tarmac again. We screeched to a halt just inches away from the man in blue.

I say, "man in blue", but his face was crimson. He was livid! He stopped the traffic in all directions and started to shout at us. I tried to explain that we thought he had waved us forward, but he wasn't listening. He then screamed, in a broad Scottish accent, "Have ye never seen a policeman before laddie?"

Mick thought for a moment and then replied, "Yes officer, but not like you."

This seemed to disarm the man, and his diatribe came to an end. As punishment he kept us standing in the middle of Princes Street for 20 minutes. We felt very humiliated as both motorists and pedestrians flowed past us. For this short time, we became yet another tourist attraction on this busy thoroughfare.

At last, our ordeal was over, and we were free to continue our journey through the city. For obvious reasons we wanted to get away as quick as possible, and the bike seemed to sense this. My rough treatment of the clutch and its fierce engagement seemed to have disabled it temporarily. The clutch lever had no effect, and we were stuck in fourth gear and unable to stop. I shouted back to Mick, "The clutch isn't working. I can't change gear or stop!" At this point we were going round a tight bend at high speed. His only comment was, "Well let's hope there's no bananas skins on the road."

Miraculously the traffic lights were kind to us, all of them being on green, and every junction seemed to clear ahead of us.

We were through Edinburgh like a dose of salts and soon found a campsite to the south of the city. The clutch started working normally again and the cause of the failure remains a mystery to this day.

That evening we found a nearby pub and had a few beers. The locals were not anti-social, but again we didn't experience the welcome we'd received at the beginning of our trip. We were just another couple of customers in a crowded pub. Walking back to the campsite we both felt a little low. Perhaps it was time to head home. Before going to sleep, we stretched out on the grass underneath the stars. We were silent for a few minutes, but the beer and the beautiful sky began to have its effect as we started getting philosophical about our trip. I told Mick that I'd got a lot to think about when I got home. Perhaps God had been speaking to me and I had to make some changes in my life. Mick certainly hadn't heard "God's Voice", but he did recognise that a few of our encounters were quite "Spooky" coincidences. He somehow knew that one day my life would head off in the Christian direction, and he wished me well.

After getting a bit emotional, like tipsy friends do, our conversation was cut short by an angry camper shouting from a nearby tent, "Can you two pipe down please. We're trying to get to sleep!"

Mick responded with his usual evening blessing, "Good Night. God Bless. Think of me when you undress." This cheeky benediction brought our evening to a close, and we were soon in our sleeping bags and fast asleep.

Chapter 4

We rose early next morning. Our intention was to ride all the way home, a distance of around 250 miles, and we didn't want to hang about. After about one hour we reached the town of Jedburgh and stopped to get some breakfast. Our knowledge of geography wasn't of a high standard, and we had to ask the café owner if we were still in Scotland. He informed us that we were in fact still north of the border, so we called in at souvenir shop and bought our mums small ornaments with Jedburgh stamped on them. These were only bits of tat, but both our mothers kept them to their dying day.

After Jedburgh we continued on the A68 towards Newcastle. I remember the road was like a giant roller coaster; one smooth hill after another. Up and down, up, and down. Mick remarked that he was feeling seasick.

At Newcastle we joined the A1 and it was plain sailing from then on. We made our usual stops every 50 miles or so, but we were soon "On the Road Again". We'd set our sights on getting home that day, and there was no point in wasting time.

Arriving back in Chesterfield in the late afternoon, we were both knackered. We'd been on the road for over 7 hours, and we were aching all over. I dropped Mick off at his house, and then rode home. My dad was at work, but my mum gave me a warm welcome. She'd had no idea about my whereabouts for the last few days. There were no mobile phones in those days, and in fact my parents didn't even have a land line. She'd learned to recognise the sound of my bike coming up the street, and she told me how relieved she'd been to hear it that day. Her prayers had been answered and I was home safe and sound.

After soaking in a hot bath for over an hour, I went downstairs to find that dad was home and there was a delicious roast dinner waiting for me. It had been a fantastic trip, but I was glad to be home.

That evening, I met up with my biker friends in the local pub. They were quite impressed by my 1200-mile trip, and I couldn't help but show off a bit about my Scottish adventure. I exaggerated some parts of the story and embellished a few facts. Fact was quickly evolving into fiction. A simple story was turning into a legend. They soaked it up and I was the centre of attention.

Walking home an empty feeling came over me. I'd been putting on an act for my mates. The real me had been lost again in the fog of my Easy Rider movie scene. But what was the "Real Me"? I had a lot thinking to do.

The summer break was coming to an end, and I was soon to return to college. I was training to be a Maths teacher, but a lot of my life didn't add up to anything meaningful. I knew that I had to change, and that the change had to be drastic. Surprisingly, during this period my life took a turn for the worse. Instead of trying to be a better person I became more immoral. You may not believe in the devil, but it seemed that he was throwing everything at me in a last-ditch effort to prevent me from becoming a true Christian. I almost lost my life on several occasions through drunkenly riding the bike or some other stupid stunts. I thought I was the life and soul of the party, always telling jokes and playing the fool. Although there was a veneer of jollity, my close friends could see through it. They would often say, "Are you ok John?", to which I would reply, "Of course I am. Why shouldn't I be."

Mick remembered this dark time, and later told me, "I'm glad you became a Christian. Even I was beginning to go off you."

My grades at college were deteriorating. Below average grades and below average life seemed to sum me up. Then they added insult to injury by saying that I needed speech therapy. My rough Derbyshire accent and my bad grammar needed sorting out. I found this very embarrassing, and of course I tried to make a joke out of it.

When they asked, "Mr Pickering, where's your grammar?", I would always reply, "She's at home with my granddad". My lecturers didn't seem to find this funny, so I was booked in to see Miss Price for elocution lessons.

I expected the lessons to be like the ones in the show "My Fair Lady". Before my first visit I even practiced saying, "The rain in Spain falls mainly on the plain!" In fact, this little ditty was never used, and Miss Price was no Professor Higgins. She was a wonderfully kind lady in her fifties. She knew how embarrassed I was to be there. I had always suffered from an inferiority complex, and the stigma of having to improve my rough speech only added to it.

Her room was like an old-fashioned Oxford Don's study. Leather armchairs and a roaring open fire. The look was completed by her pet Spaniel asleep by the hearth. Miss Price gently diagnosed my speech problems, and then the lessons became more like counselling sessions. By the second session I was pouring my heart out to her. I told her that my life was in a real mess. I told her that I had a Christian background but just couldn't live the life. She then told me that she was a Christian and would pray for me. Another one of those "spooky" coincidences!

During my final lesson with Miss Price, she asked me what my plan was for the future. I told her that I wasn't going to rush into some fake conversion. I'd tried this in the past – saying "the sinner's prayer" and then, after a few weeks, reverting to my former life. I was now counting the cost of discipleship before taking my final step of commitment. She said that she thought this was a good plan and remarked that this approach concurred with Jesus' teaching on the subject. She then did what no other lecturer had ever done. She gently placed her hand on my shoulder and prayed for me. I'm sure that in these modern times the thought police would declare this highly irregular, but for me it was wonderful. As this little, middle-aged lady prayed for me I felt a feeling of warmth and power flood through me. This was one more important piece in the jig saw of my life. The full picture was coming together.

That Christmas was the last pagan festival that I celebrated. I did attend church, but the festive period was also filled with drunken parties and riotous behaviour. There was one big difference, however. This time my heart wasn't in it. I looked at my fellow revellers and realised I didn't fit in anymore. It all seemed empty to me. I wanted something deeper from these shallow celebrations. Suddenly I knew it wouldn't be so hard to give up this lifestyle.

A few months later I went to a Sunday evening church service with my parents. I couldn't wait for the service to end, because I'd arranged to meet a bunch of mates in town. On arriving home, I quickly changed from my "Sunday Best" into my biker gear and set off on the bike. I wasn't very happy as it started to drizzle. It wouldn't be too great sitting in the pub with wet jeans.

As I rounded a bend, I noticed a group of people standing by the side of the road, and a smashed-up motorcycle on the grass verge. I pulled to a stop, put my bike on its stand and went to investigate. In the centre of the crowd a young man was lying in the gutter. He looked badly injured. It seemed that a motorist had pulled out of the junction directly in front of the motorcyclist. The man had hit the car head on. The foursome from the car made the excuse that they hadn't seen him coming. The two girls kept saying, "I hope he's alright. Oh, I hope he's alright."

He wasn't "alright". He was fatally injured. An off-duty nurse arrived on the scene and tried to help him as best as she could. She asked the onlookers if anyone had a coat to put over him. The crowd all seemed to be well dressed. I imagined some of them were on their way home from church, while the others were on their way to a night out on the town. No one volunteered a coat. I decided to put my short leather jacket over him as we waited for the ambulance. It was a pathetic sight. A young man dying in the gutter with a scruffy leather jacket thrown over him, and the miserable drizzle falling incessantly.

At last, the ambulance arrived. The medics threw my jacket to one side as they checked him over. I picked it up and noticed that the lining was soaked in blood. As I looked down on that young man, I saw myself lying there. We were of a similar age travelling in opposite directions on the same road. Like a mirror image. It could so easily have been me dying in the gutter. There but by the grace of God.

I was shaken to the core. I knew I wasn't prepared for death. Neither was I prepared for life. In fact, my life was a sham. It couldn't stand the test of time or eternity.

I abandoned my night out and returned home. When I removed my blood-soaked jacket, my shirt was also stained with blood. My mother gasped, thinking I was badly injured. I quickly explained what had happened and she told me to remove my shirt and soak it in a bath of cold water. The water turned pink. That young man's blood was part of my redemption.

A short time later, just before my twentieth birthday, my mother arranged for me to go away with a bunch of young Christians to the Yorkshire Dales. I wasn't very pleased about this, but then I found out that the France brothers were helping to organise the trip. These three young men were good fun to be with and I really admired them as Christians. I somehow knew that the short Easter break would not be boring. My mother knew it would do me good to mix with Christians like them, and she had already paid the deposit. As I had caused her a great deal of heartache in the past I agreed to go.

When I arrived at the place, I tried to look hard, dressed in my biker's jacket and a cigarette dangling from my mouth. No one seemed that impressed. They just accepted me as I was. I found this strange, but I soon settled down and had a great time hiking and swimming with the other young people. They were full of life and seemed genuinely happy. No one was getting drunk, or taking drugs, but perhaps they had what I was looking for.

They held meetings twice a day and I sensed something powerful and moving each time they met. I stuck out like a sore thumb. All around me young people were enjoying worshipping Jesus, while I remained cool and observed them objectively as an outsider. They appeared to know and love God with all their hearts; I merely knew about Him in my head.

After every meeting I would go for a smoke and think deeply about the Christian faith. I weighed it all up in my mind, and I knew that my whole life would have to change. Lots of things would have to go, for I couldn't have the new life without letting go of the old. I had tried a watered-down version of Christianity and it had failed. Now I knew that it was all or nothing. Was I going to be boss of my life or was Jesus going to be Lord.

I asked one of the France brothers what made his faith different to mine. He said that he didn't know what kind of faith I had. All he could say was that he had given his whole life to Christ unreservedly, and as a result Christ had poured His life into him. It made sense – these young people seemed literally full of Jesus and their lives reflected this.

I finally made my decision as I was travelling home in a car with a group of Christians. The driver suggested that we had a prayer time. As we were travelling at 60mph down the A1, I was a bit nervous that he would close his eyes whilst praying. I genuinely wondered whether these Christians were that crazy.

All the Christians prayed (without crashing) and then it was my turn. There was a pregnant pause while I thought things over. A shopping list of things popped up in my mind. A list of things that I knew must go. I had no confidence that I could conquer all this junk, but then I felt the voice of God speaking in my inner being. "Don't worry about that list. Just give yourself wholly to me and I will deal with the list." I could almost see the hand of God tearing it up and scattering it to the wind.

I was still nervous of taking that final step, but it was time to do it. "O Lord," I said out loud, "I'm giving You my whole life. I want to be Your disciple. Please forgive my sin and accept me. I've messed up twenty years of my life trying to run it myself, but now I'm handing it over to You. I want You to be my Lord".

I can't describe how I felt as I prayed. God seemed so real to me that my whole body seemed to be thrilled with the experience. I had come to Him on His terms not mine, and His Holy Spirit had filled me. The old clay pot of my life was running over with a heart-warming divine wine.

I can't say all my problems ended on that day, but I do know that I became a new person. I literally felt "Born Again". When I arrived home my mother had a new son. Her faithful prayers had been answered.

A few weeks later I had a serious accident on the bike. The car in front of me suddenly came to an abrupt halt. I slammed on the brakes and went into a sliding skid. My back wheel hit the rear of his car and the bike flipped over. I was flung through the air and did a full somersault before landing on my back on the wrong side of the road. Fortunately, the driver coming the other way pulled to a halt just inches away from me. Miraculously I sustained only minor injuries. I couldn't say the same for my brand-new pair of Levi jeans. They were hanging in shreds.

The driver that I had collided with initially showed concern for me, but when he saw that I wasn't badly injured his mood changed. He started shouting that my reckless driving had damaged his precious new car. I asked him why he had stopped so suddenly with no apparent reason. This made him even more angry. "Oh, now you're blaming me, are you?" he shouted. I decided it was pointless arguing. I was hurting from the grazing (gravel rash) and the bruising, and I looked a right Charlie standing in the middle of the road with my backside hanging out.

We exchanged details and he drove away, as I picked up the bike and pushed it to the side of the road. It was badly dented, and the high, cow-horn handlebars were now looking like dropped racing bars. Surprisingly it started second kick, as always, and I decided that I could ride it home laying on the tank using my new style handlebars. The clutch lever had broken off, but I knew that with a push I could crash it into second and crawl home without changing gear (or stopping).

As I was working all this out, a little old lady came out of a nearby bungalow and offered me a needle and thread to make myself decent. I explained that I couldn't sew and asked if she had any safety pins. With her help I pinned my jeans together and created a new fashion that the Punk Rockers would adopt years later.

With the engine running two beefy men pushed me down the road. Judging the speed and revs to be about right, I forced it into second gear. My plan worked and I was on my way. I was only 2 miles from home, and I made the journey without further incidents.

That accident ended my biking career for the time being. It wasn't long after this that I met Margaret and fell in love. A year later I got a full-time teaching job and bought my first car. After that we were married and soon started a family. As many young men find out, motorcycles must go on the back burner when family commitments, utility bills and mortgages come along.

It was 1972 when my young biking days came to an end. However, in the same year a beautiful 500cc Triumph Daytona was just coming off the production line in Coventry. Little did I know that this machine was destined to be mine nearly forty years later. God works in mysterious ways!

Chapter 5

Actually, it was 38 years before I owned my next bike. This may seem like a long time, but this wasn't a period of arid, bike less desert. It wasn't my personal Forty Years in the Wilderness. God had replaced my love of motorcycles with a love for Him and a love for my wife and kids. Life was filled with activity. I had a full-time teaching position. Instead of teaching maths I had switched to teaching Religious Education and really enjoyed my job. I ran a successful Sunday School and a Youth Group. As my preaching skills developed, I was invited to speak in different churches around the area. I didn't care which denomination the church was and preached the same Biblical gospel message everywhere I went.

Playing the guitar and writing Christian songs also became an important part of my life. I performed at small gigs all over the country and produced several CDs. You can listen to these humble offerings on Spotify etc. Just type in "John Pickering Christian Singer".

For many years I was involved in street evangelism. Every Friday or Saturday night I would stand outside the town centre pubs trying to spread the gospel. A small, dedicated team helped me with this work. We even ran a coffee bar which provided free coffee along with Christian counselling.

Yes, my life was full of activity, but not at the expense of my family life. I always had time for Margaret and my two children, Wesley and Rebecca. One of my favourite verses in the Bible is 2 Samuel 2:30, "Those who honour me I will honour."

God is no man's debtor. Whatever I gave to Him, He more than compensated with His gifts to me.

When the children had left home and I retired from teaching, I had a little more time on my hands. I discovered that the church that I grew up in was in danger of closing. God spoke to me in a very clear way, and I knew that I had to offer my services as voluntary pastor. We now have a church that is not closing, and God has provided a wonderful group of Christian friends who work so hard to maintain this gospel outpost.

Where do motorcycles fit into all this? Well, I can't prove this, but I believe that God has allowed me to take up where I left off 38 years before. Late in life I kicked up my old love of bikes. My brother-in-law, Tony agreed to sell me his vintage Triumph Daytona. I was a little rusty, both in my riding and my mechanic skills, but I was a quick learner. I also gained two new friends who were superb motorcycle mechanics. Pete Harding was in his eighties. We all called him "Uncle Pete", and his skills were unbelievable. He had his own lathe and other engineering equipment and could make his own parts. He had rebuilt several vintage bikes, the oldest being a 1920 Triumph 350cc. All his bikes looked like they had just come out of the showroom. Even in his eighties he still rode all of them in turn.

My 1972 Triumph Daytona 500cc

The other friend was an ex-pupil of mine called Russ. I call him "The Bike Whisperer". He can take any engine and miraculously bring it back to life. I have seen with my own eyes some of these "miracles". A rust bucket would arrive that hadn't run for many years. Within an hour the old engine would burst into life, accompanied by a load a of smoke and a cheer.

With the help of these two artisans, I have been privileged in my latter years to own and renovate at least ten machines. These bikes have not been "gods", they have been hobbies. Hobbies that have not interfered with my work for Christ. I thank God for allowing me such pleasure in later life. Not only have I enjoyed working on them, but I have enjoyed riding them. Riding down the road I feel eighteen again. It's only when I remove my crash helmet and look in the mirror that I realise that I am just an old fool reliving my youth.

Of all my recent bikes, one stands out as really special. It was delivered to my house at the start of the covid lockdown and was my redemption during those isolated months.

Russ came around to view the machine. He couldn't wait to get the old girl running. Working together we connected a new battery, cleaned and set the points, wired brushed the spark plug, changed the oil and then poured fresh petrol into the carburettor. It started second kick, as always! In less than an hour we had poured new life into this dead collection of metal. It was like witnessing a resurrection.

The "rust bucket" as it arrived at our house.

Fortunately, the weather was extremely good, so I spent most of summer outdoors working on transforming this old rust bucket into a thing of beauty. The bike happened to be the same make and model that Mick and I had ridden around Scotland four decades earlier. Yes, it was a 1965 Royal Enfield Crusader Sports 250cc single cylinder.

This motorcycle has become very important to me. It brings back such great memories. It reminds me of Mick Collins, and more than any other bike takes me back to my days of youth. In a few months it became my pride and joy. I still work on it, doing fine adjustments and replacing parts here and there, but it is essentially complete.

The transformed 1965 Royal Enfield Crusader Sports

I don't think I'll ever part with this nostalgic piece of machinery. Even when I'm too old to ride it I will still polish it and kick her up now and again. When I'm too old to polish and kick

I'll just look at her and remember the good old days of freedom and youth. When I'm dead they can bury me with her!

Maybe you want to know what happened to Mick Collins. We remained best friends until his death in 2017, spending time together talking about old times and putting the world to rights. We never tired of telling the same old jokes and telling the same old stories. He never became a Christian, although it wasn't for lack of trying. He once asked me if I still prayed for him every day. I was embarrassed to tell him that I had given up. Mick replied, "I hope God hasn't given up."

When he was diagnosed with terminal cancer, I promised I would stick with him to the bitter end. He told me he was thankful for that but made me promise not to try and force a death bed conversion on him. His exact words were, "I don't want you hovering over me like some religious vulture."

I kept my promise to him. When I was called to his bedside in his final hours, I was desperate to hear him make his peace with God. I gently asked him if he wanted to pray. He thought for a moment and then politely replied, "No thanks John. I don't think so."

Instead of praying I helped him smoke his last cigarette and then he slipped peacefully away. I sobbed as I realised I had finally been separated from this life-long friend.

I was honoured to take Mick's funeral and the service was packed to the walls. I couldn't resist briefly relating the story of the Scottish trip. I told the congregation how I had longed for Mick to become a Christian. I knew that he could have been so effective as a man of God. But it wasn't to be. I had chosen the Christian path through life. Mick had chosen a different route. But through it all we had remained so close as friends.

When my turn comes to die, I only hope that I can face it with courage and humour in the same way as Mick. Until then I hope I can keep on riding. Riding with confidence into the sunset.

❈

Poetry in Motion

These are three songs that I wrote around the time of the Scotland trip.
(You can listen to 'Death Looked Down' on Spotify)

North up to Gretna

I woke up that morning as the sun began to shine,
I kicked up the bike and I decided to ride,
Going north up to Gretna I cut of west to the coast,
And I don't know which part I enjoyed the most.

My friend was riding behind me, and the sun was high,
We didn't know just where we were bound,
We just kept on moving, we were riding all of the day,
No one place could ever tie us down.

We saw the people of the city and it made us glad we were free,
The sights of the city never look too pretty to me,
We got out of that dirty old town just as quickly as everyone should,
And we'll never go back there even if we could.

Soon we were out in the country lanes again,
With the rocks and the trees and the birds and the bees and the sky,
And if you don't believe in God my friend, I wish you could have been there,
For His handiwork was right before our eyes.

Death Looked Down

As I rode out on that stormy night,
Looking for my share of fun,
I saw a boy who'd been knocked off his bike,
Lying in the road cold and numb.

I knelt down to his cold blue lips,
To hear what he had to say,
"Please tell my mother that I died quick,
Don't let her know I went this way".

Death looked down on the street that day,
Death looked down as I heard him say,
"Oh God have mercy on my soul,
God have mercy on my soul."

He gave a sigh, and then he died,
But nobody seemed to care.
As I looked down on that poor young man,
I saw myself lying there.

Now I think I'm a man, but try as I can,
The tears they still well up in me,
When I think of that boy dying in the road,
When he was just trying to be free.

You can't make Four Wheels Better than Two.

With the sun in my face and breathing fresh air,
I'm riding along without a care,
The sound of the engine drumming in my ears,
Makes all other sounds of the world disappear.

With the engine humming and the wheels turning,
My heart for the road is forever yearning,
No, my friend, no matter what you do,
You can't make four wheels better than two.

The guy in the car may be warm and dry,
But I like riding underneath the sky,
They'd like to drive us off of every highway,
But they're just jealous they can't have it my way.

With the engine humming and the wheels turning,
My heart for the road is forever yearning,
No, my friend, no matter what you do,
You can't make four wheels better than two.

Well, I've had my excitement and I've had my thrills.
I've had my near misses and I've had my spills,
But you'll never cage me in behind a load of tin,
For to cage a free bird is such a sin.

With the engine humming and the wheels turning,
My heart for the road is forever yearning,
No, my friend, no matter what you do,
You can't make four wheels better than two.

Gallery of My Recent Bikes

1972 Triumph Daytona 500cc

Yamaha Virago 535

Yamaha Virago 1100cc

Honda 185cc Twin

Yamaha DT1 250 Two Stroke

Yamaha 650 cc

Herald 125cc

Royal Enfield Crusader Sports 250cc Trials

Beta Trials Bike 250cc

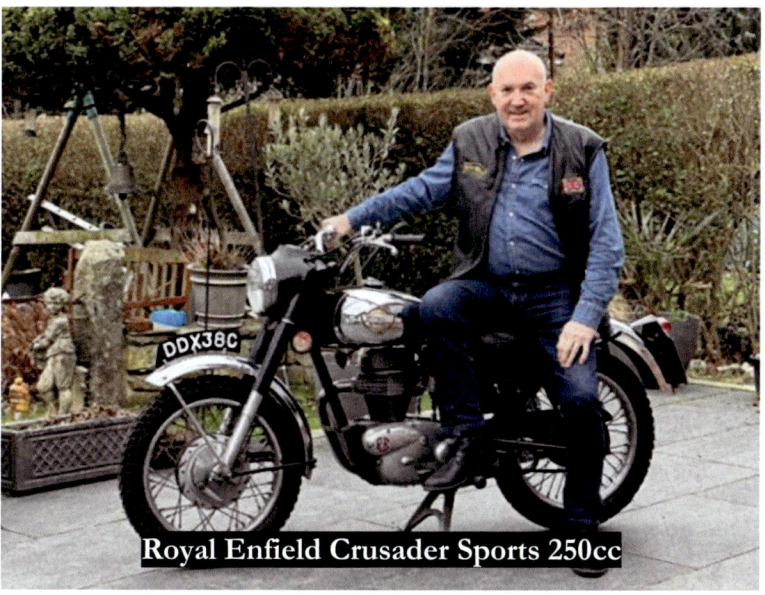

Royal Enfield Crusader Sports 250cc

Herald Classic 250cc

50cc Chinese Scooter

Mini Moto

Next generation bikers? My grand-children Matilda and Noah.

Printed and bound by CPI Group (UK) Ltd, Croydon, CR0 4YY